First Japanese Reader: A Beginner's Dual-language Book

Copyright © 2017

All rights reserved.

CONTENTS

	Preface	1
1	かさじぞう	2
2	Kasajizou	5
3	Vocabulary and Gloss	7
4	子育て幽霊	27
5	The Child-rearing Ghost	30
6	Vocabulary and Gloss	33
7	雪女	47
8	The Snow Woman	49
9	Vocabulary and Gloss	51
10	猫の茶わん	66
11	The Cat's Teacup	68
12	Vocabulary and Gloss	70
13	大工と三毛猫	82
14	The Carpenter and the Calico Cat	84
15	Vocabulary and Gloss	86

Audio for the stories can be found on the
LEARN JAPANESE Youtube Channel:
https://www.youtube.com/channel/
UCtCvCVxgHKWSO086z78EObw/videos

PREFACE

In order to make language learning logical and simple, the reading material in textbooks is usually quite dull. And most textbooks don't teach much about the writing style of novels and short stories. This means that even an intermediate student of Japanese might encounter many difficulties when attempting to explore Japanese literature. This book is aimed at students who wish to bridge this gap between real Japanese literature and the reading material of textbooks.

This book will also help students learn or solidify a lot of the grammar required to pass level N4 of the Japanese Language Proficiency Test as well as expand their vocabulary, because while the stories in this collection are based on stories from Japanese folklore, they have been written in a more accessible manner and with common words.

Each story is presented first in Japanese followed by an English translation. Yet, the English version is more literal than might be found in a stand-alone translation in order to help the reader better understand its connection with the Japanese.

Following this, the story will be divided into smaller sections where each new word is defined and explanations of the grammar involved are given. However, explanations of elementary particles like は, が, で, に, を, も, etc. will not be given and words will only be defined once in each story. Explanations of each aspect of grammar will also only be given once and the stories become progressively more difficult, so the reader is encouraged to read them in order.

There will also occasionally be "Cultural Notes" that explain certain aspects of Japanese culture that are relevant to the story.

かさじぞう

　昔々、小さい村の近くにおじいさんとおばあさんが住んでいました。二人は心優しいだけどひどく貧乏でした。
　ある年の大晦日のことです。
　明日はお正月だから、おじいさんとおばあさんはお正月のおモチを食べたいです。でも、新年を迎えるための米一粒でさえ買うことできない状態でした。そこで、二人でカサを作りました。それを小さい村で売って、お正月のおモチを買うつもりなんです。
　やがて、おじいさんは「カサは五つがあるから、モチぐらいを買えるはずだ」と言いました。
　おばあさんはおじいさんを見送りました。
　「もうすぐ雪が降りそうだ。気をつけてくださいよ」と言いました。
　おじいさんは五つのカサを持って、出かけました。小さい村へ向かいました。家を出てまもなく、真っ白な雪が降ってきました。雪はだんだん激しくなったので、おじいさんは村へ急ぎました。小さい村の前におじぞうさまが六つ並んで立っていました。おじぞうさまは頭にも肩にも雪が厚く積もっていました。
　これを見たおじいさんは止まりました。

「おじぞうさま。雪が降っています。このカサを被ってください」と言いました。
　おじいさんはおじぞうさまの頭の上に売るつもりのカサを被せてやりました。ところが、最後のおじぞうさまの前にきた時、おじいさんはもう持っているカサがないことに気がつきました。
　「はて、困った…」
　ふと思いついて、自分の頭の上に被っていたカサを脱ぎました。
　「このカサは古いですけれど」と言い、被せてやりました。
　そして、急いで頭を手で覆いながら、おじいさんは家に帰りました。
　おばあさんはおじいさんが濡れて帰ってきたのを見て、びっくりしていました。
　「何が起こったの？おじいさんのカサはどこですか」と聞きました。
　おじいさんはおばあさんにおじぞうさまの話をしました。
　「それは良いことをしましたね。まあまあ、おモチなんて、なくてもいいですよ」
　おばあさんはニコニコして言いました。
　おじいさんのしたことを一緒に喜びました。しかし、食べ物や飲み物がなくなってしまっていました。そこで、二人は薄い布団に包まって、早く寝てしまいました。

　その夜、激しく降る雪がますます積もりました。
　夜中におじいさんとおばあさんはふと目を覚ましました。不思議な声が「じいさんの家はどこだ？じいさんの家はどこだ？」と歌いました。その声は、にぎやかで楽しそうな歌声です。どうやら二人の家に向かってやってくるような様子です。歌声はどんどん近づいて、とうとう二人の家の前までくると、何か重いものを置く音がしました。それから声は消えてしまいました。

二人はそっと戸を開けて、じっと見ていました。雪はすでに止んでいて、あたりには月の光が明るく輝きました。遠くにカサを被ったおじぞうさまが帰っていくのが見えました。
　　そして、家の前にはお正月のおモチが山のように置いてありました。

KASAJIZOU

Once upon a time, an old man and an old woman lived near a small village. The couple was kind-hearted, but terribly poor.

It all happened one New Year's Eve.

Since tomorrow was New Year's Day, the old man and the old woman wanted to eat rice cakes for the New Year. But in their situation they couldn't afford even one grain of rice to greet the new year. Therefore the two made straw hats that they intended to sell so they could buy New Year's rice cakes.

Before long, the old man said, "We have five hats, so we ought to be able to buy some rice cakes."

The old woman saw the old man off.

"It looks like it will snow soon. Please be careful," the old woman said.

The old man left, carrying the five straw hats and headed toward the small village. Soon after he left, pure white snow began to fall. The snow gradually became more intense, so the old man hurried. Before the small village, six Jizou stood in a row. On both their heads and their shoulders, snow was piling up thickly.

When he saw this, the old man stopped in his tracks.

The old man took the hats he had intended to sell and covered the heads of the Jizou. However, when he came before the last Jizou, the old man realized he didn't have any more hats.

"Oh dear, this won't do…"

Suddenly he was struck with an idea and removed the hat he was wearing on his own head.

"This hat is old, but…" he said and placed it on the Jizou.

Then the old man hurriedly headed home, covering his head with his hand.

The old woman was astonished to see the old man return home soaking wet.

"Did something happen? Where is your hat?" she asked.

The old man told her of the Jizou.

"That is a good thing you did. Well, we can do without the rice cakes," the old woman smiled and said.

They rejoiced at the thing the old man had done. But, regrettably, they had nothing to eat or drink so the couple wrapped up in their thin futon and went to bed early.

That night, the fiercely falling snow piled up more and more.

At midnight, the old man and the old woman suddenly awoke. Mysterious voices were singing, "Oh where, oh where is the old man's house?" The voices sounded lively and merry and seemed to be coming toward the couple's house. The singing voices came closer and closer until they reached the front of the house and there came the sound of something heavy being put down. After that, the voices completed disappeared.

The couple softly opened the door and stared. The snow had already stopped and all around sparkled brightly in the light of the moon. In the distance, they saw Jizou wearing straw hats walking away.

And there, in front of their house, was piled a mountain of rice cakes for New Year's.

VOCABULARY AND GLOSS

　昔々、小さい村の近くにおじいさんとおばあさんが住んでいました。二人は心優しいだけどひどく貧乏でした。

　　昔々【むかしむかし】 once upon a time, long ago
　　小さい村【ちいさいむら】 a small village
　　近く【ちかく】 near
　　おじいさん old man
　　おばあさん old woman
　　住む【すむ】 to live, reside
　　二人【ふたり】 two people, couple
　　心優しい【こころやさしい】 kind-hearted
　　けど but
　　ひどく terribly, extremely
　　貧乏【びんぼう】 poor, destitute

　昔々 or just 昔 is the classic opening to Japanese folktales just like "Once upon a time..." is the classic opening in English. 小さい村の近く is a post-positional phrase and since it is followed by に, it is acting as an adverbial phrase and thus modifying the verb. Therefore it is describing where the couple lives and does not mean *"The small village near the old man and woman."

　The second sentence is a compound sentence combining 二人は心優しいでした and 　二人はひどく貧乏でした. However, since one description is positive and the other is negative, て-form is not used and these phrases are instead connected by けど. ひどく is simply the adverb-form of ひどい. Adverbs can be made from い-adjectives simply by replacing い with く.

ある年の大晦日のことです。
　明日はお正月だから、おじいさんとおばあさんはお正月のおモチを食べたいです。

　　　ある年【あるとし】one year, a certain year
　　　大晦日【おおみそか】New Year's Eve
　　　こと event, occurrence
　　　明日【あした】tomorrow
　　　お正月【おしょうがつ】New Year's Day
　　　から since, because
　　　おモチ sticky rice cake
　　　食べたい【たべたい】to want to eat

　ある is a noun modifier used when referring to an unspecific time, place, thing, etc. It might help to think of ある年 as meaning, "a year that exists."
　This is a sentence with an unstated subject. The main phrase is just ことです with the rest of the sentence consisting of a phrase modifying こと. Sentences that modify こと are often used in Japanese as a way to introduce what is about to be told.
　Notice also that this sentence is in non-past tense even though the story takes place in the past. Non-past tense is conventionally used in Japanese to provide commentary to a story, as it does in this sentence. Another way it is used is to express what is on the main character's mind, as it does in the second sentence.
　The second sentence is another compound sentence connected this time with から. Since から is a particle, the phrase that it attaches to is always the explanation. 食べたい is the たい-form of the verb 食べる; adding たい to the stem form of a verb changes the meaning to, "want to [verb]" and can be used and conjugated as an い-adjective. And, as noted above, since this sentence expresses what is on the main characters' minds (what they want to eat) it is in non-past tense.

でも、新年を迎えるための米一粒でさえ買うことできない状態でした。

でも but
新年【しんねん】new year
迎える【むかえる】to welcome, go out to meet
ため for
米【こめ】rice
一粒【ひとつぶ】one grain
さえ even
買う【かう】ことできない cannot buy
状態【じょうたい】the situation, state

The second sentence is similar to the sentence before the last one where the main phrase is simply 状態でした with the rest of the sentence being a phrase modifying 状態. So this ending gives the sentence the meaning, "The situation was…" These little surprise endings make Japanese more difficult to read for English speakers, but after enough exposure, they're not so surprising.

The phrase that modifies 状態 begins with 新, which is a prefix that can be added to nouns with the meaning of "neo-" or "new." It also contains the very helpful noun, ため. When ため is linked to a noun phrase with の, it describes the purpose of that noun phrase. The purpose is whatever phrase modifies ため, which in this story is 新年を迎える "welcome the new year." And ため is linked to the noun phrase 米一粒 "one grain of rice." So, 新年を迎えるための米一粒 becomes one giant noun phrase saying, "one grain of rice to welcome the new year." And this noun phrase is followed by the particle でさえ, which simply means "even."

Two more examples of this use of ため are 勉強するための時間がある, meaning, "There is time to study," and 読むための本がほしい, meaning, "[Sub] wants a book to read." We wouldn't want to say 勉強する時間 or 読む本 because these phrases would mean something like "time that studies" and "a book that reads."

And at the end of this phrase, 買う is followed by こと できない. When こと(が)できる is added to a verb, it has the same meaning as the potential form of that verb. They are pretty much interchangeable and both are used in everyday speech; however, when people are speaking of things they are physically unable to do, it seems to be more common to use ことでき ない rather than the negative potential form (買えない in this case).

Cultural Notes:

Mochi is a gluey substance made from rice and molded into small balls. It is often sold in ice cream shops and cafes, but is also a traditional food eaten to celebrate New Year's. Since mochi itself is bland, it is frequently stuffed with a sweet filling.

Japan used to celebrate the New Year at the same time as the Chinese New Year, but in 1873 (5 years after the Meiji Restoration) the date was changed to January 1.

そこで、二人でカサを作りました。それを小さい村で売って、お正月のおモチを買うつもりなんです。

そこで therefore, so
カサ a conical straw hat
作る 【つくる】 to make
売る 【うる】 to sell
つもり intention
ん explanatory particle

Here, the second sentence is an explanation for the first, answering the unstated question for why the couple is making hats. It is the ん particle which indicates that this sentence is an explanation (this particle has pretty much the same meaning as から). So, here we have yet another example where the main phrase is simply, んです. Now, when です/だ precedes the ex-planatory particle ん, it changes to な. So instead of *つもりだ んです the grammatically correct usage is つもりなんです. つもり is a noun that means "intention" and when it is modified by a phrase, it forms a noun phrase that tells what the subject intends to do. Thus the ending つもりなんです gives the sentence the meaning, "Because the [subject] intends to…" This sentence also contains a て-form used to link a sequence of events. So both these actions describe what the old man intends to do and this sentence means something like, "Because the couple intends to sell them [the hats] in the small village and buy New Year's rice cakes."

And here again, since this sentence expresses what is on the main characters' minds (what they intend to do) it is in non-past tense. However, note also that つもり is also followed by the non-past tense of です/だ. This has nothing to do with commentary or expressing the main characters' thoughts. When つもり is followed by the past tense copula でした/だった, it means something like, "had intended to…" or "believed that…" For example, 医者になるつもりだった means, "I intended to become a doctor," and in both languages there is the implication that the person speaking didn't become a doctor. When つもり is followed by the non-past tense of です/だ it tells of the subject's plans for the future.

Cultural Note:

A カサ(written in kanji as 笠) is a conical hat worn in many Asian countries to protect from the elements. They are often made of straw or bamboo.

やがて、おじいさんは「カサは五つがあるから、モチぐらいを買えるはずだ」と言いました。
　おばあさんはおじいさんを見送りました。
　「もうすぐ雪が降りそうだ。気をつけてくださいよ」と言いました。

やがて before long
五つ【いつつ】five
ぐらい *see below
買える to be able to buy
はず *see below
言う【いう】to say
見送る【みおくる】to see off
もうすぐ very soon
雪【ゆき】snow
降る【ふる】to precipitate
気【き】をつける to be careful, take care

　The first sentence gives a standard example of a quotation and we will see several variations throughout this book. The suffix ぐらい basically makes the word it follows less specific. It is used here to mean "some" or "a few." And here 買う is in potential form, so it takes on the meaning "to be able to buy." This modifies はず, which is a noun that is sometimes a challenge to translate because it doesn't have a good English equivalent. It is used to indicate that the phrase that modifies it is a belief or expectation that the subject has (which might or might not be valid); so "ought" was used in the translation to convey this meaning. In general, はず makes the statement that modifies it less certain.
　The word もう has several different meanings, two of which we will see in this story. Here it is used to mean "in a short time."
　With the verb 見送る, the person who is leaving takes the を particle and the person seeing them off is the subject, so

they take either は or が. 降る is an intransitive verb, so whatever is precipitating does not take the を particle and takes either は or が.

And in the final sentence here, the suffix そうな is attached to the verb 降る. When verbs and adjectives in stem-form are followed by そうな, the combination conveys the meaning that something *looks like, sounds like,* or *seems to have* the property of the stem-form word. For example, おいしそう means "looks delicious" and in the above sentence, 雪が降りそう means, "It looks like snow." The whole combination functions like a な-adjective.

おじいさんは五つのカサを持って、出かけました。小さい村へ向かいました。家を出てまもなく、真っ白な雪が降ってきました。

    持つ【もつ】to carry, possess
    出かける【でかける】to leave, depart
    向かう【むかう】to go toward
    家【いえ】house
    出る【でる】to exit, leave
    まもなく soon
    真っ白な【まっしろな】pure white

The particle へ is similar to but vaguer than the に particle. The に particle indicates a final destination, while with the へ particle there is no guarantee that the subject will reach the indicated destination only that it is the general direction the subject is moving in. The difference between に and へ is similar to the difference between "to" and "toward."

まもなく is the adverb form of 間もない (lit. "there is no interval"). This phrase is heard on trains in Japan just before each stop to announce which station the train will *soon* arrive at.

真っ is added to some nouns and adjectives to add a meaning like "total" or "complete" to them. For example, 真っ黒な = pitch black; 真っ直ぐ = straight ahead; 真っ昼間 = broad daylight.

This sentence ends with the verb 降る paired with the auxiliary (helping) verb くる (to come). This auxiliary verb has many different uses (as we will see throughout this book), but the way it is used here is to signal a change in state. So 雪が降ってきました signals that the weather went from not snowing to snowing—in other words, it began to snow (the precipitation "came").

雪はだんだん激しくなったので、おじいさんは村へ急ぎました。小さい村の前におじぞうさまが六つ並んで立っていました。

だんだん gradually
激しい【はげしい】intense, furious
なる to become
ので because
急ぐ【いそぐ】to hurry
前【まえ】before
おじぞうさま *see below
六つ【むっつ】six
並ぶ【ならぶ】to stand in a line, line up
立つ【たつ】to stand

Here we have the first occurrence of 擬態語 (ぎたいご), mimetic words. These words usually have a repeated sound or two similar sounds. They are often used adverbially to make impressionistic expressions. Mimetic adverbs can act as adverbs by either standing alone (as だんだん does here) or by being

15

followed by the と particle. There are several more in this story (all of which stand alone).

When an い-adjective is used with the verb なる, the い is replaced with く.

並んで立っていました doesn't mean "lined up and were standing." 並んで is used adverbially to mean "side by side," so 並んで立っていました means "stood in a row." Similarly, 並んで歩いた means "walked side by side" and not "lined up and walked." There are a couple more verbs that act this way in the story.

おじぞうさまは頭にも肩にも雪が厚く積もっていました。

これを見たおじいさんは止まりました。

頭【あたま】head
肩【かた】shoulders
厚い【あつい】deep, thick
積もる【つもる】to pile up, accumulate
見る【みる】to see
止まる【とまる】to stop (moving)

When も follows each noun in a list, it has the same function as と ("and"), but with more emphasis. It has the same function as the usual usage of も, except here each item is mentioned in the same sentence and both are followed by も (instead of just the second item). Thus when も is used in this way, it is usually translated as, "both…and…"

The second sentence begins with an alternative way of describing a sequence of events in Japanese. Instead of saying something like これを見た時、おじいさんは止まりました or おじいさんはこれを見て、止まりました the subject of the sentence can just be modified. This is often used in Japanese writing and makes for very compact sentences.

Cultural Note:
Stop signs in Japan say 止まれ, which is the imperative form of 止まる, commanding drivers to stop.

「おじぞうさま。雪が降っています。このカサを被ってください」と言いました。
おじいさんはおじぞうさまの頭の上に売るつもりのカサを被せてやりました。

上【うえ】over, on top
被る【かぶる】to put on (one's head)
被せる【かぶせる】to put on (someone else's head), cover (with)

The second sentence here might look a little complicated, but it is basically just the sentence おじいさんはカサを被せてやりました combined with two modifying phrases: おじぞうさまの頭の上に and 売るつもりのカサ.

The verb 被せる is used with the auxiliary (helping) verb やる= "to give." てやる is a more casual version of てあげる but has the same meaning: that the verb was done as a favor for someone else (the subject "gives the doing of" the verb). So the old man is doing the Jizou the favor of putting hats on them.

The phrase おじぞうさまの頭の上に is another postpositional phrase followed by に, so we know that it modifies the verb 被せる: it tells us where the old man puts the hats. The phrase おじぞうさまの頭の上 basically means "on top of/over the Jizou's heads."

And in the final modifier, we see the noun つもり again, which is modified by 売る to mean "intends to sell." And this noun phrase is connected to カサ with the の particle to create a bigger noun phrase: 売るつもりのカサ meaning, "the hats [he] intends to sell."

ところが、最後のおじぞうさまの前にきた時、おじいさんはもう持っているカサがないことに気がつきました。

　　ところが however
　　最後【さいご】last
　　くる to come
　　〜時【とき】when...
　　もう more, another
　　持つ【もつ】to have, possess
　　こと *see below
　　気【き】がつく to realize, notice

　This sentence can also be broken down like the last. The main sentence is essentially: おじいさんはことに気がつきました。And 最後のおじぞうさまの前にきた時 and もう持っているカサがない are modifying phrases.

　気がつく is a common expression that can be used like a verb. The noun phrase that is "realized" or "noticed" is indicated by the に particle. However, the old man realizes もう持っているカサがない, which is a verb phrase. Thus こと is added to the end of this phrase so that it can be used in a noun phrase slot. こと simply nominalizes the phrase and really doesn't have a meaning here, but can be thought of as meaning, "the fact that…" or "the circumstance that..."

　Here is the second usage of もう with a different meaning from the first. In conjunction with ない, it indicates that, of the hats that the man had (持っているカサ), there are no more.

　The last modifier is an adverbial phrase consisting of the noun 時 preceded by a modifying phrase. So it basically means "the time that…" but is usually translated as "when…" And the modifying phrase of 時 contains yet another post-positional phrase followed　by に: 最後のおじぞうさまの前に. This　phrase modifies the verb くる, so it is indicating that the old man "came before the last Jizou." Thus the entire adverbial phrase means, "when (he) came before the last Jizou."

「はて、困った...」
　ふと思いついて、自分の頭の上に被っていたカサを脱ぎました。
「このカサは古いですけれど」と言い、被せてやりました。
　そして、急いで頭を手で覆いながら、おじいさんは家に帰りました。

はて Oh dear! Goodness!
困る【こまる】this won't do
ふと suddenly
思いつく【おもいつく】to be struck with an idea
自分 oneself
脱ぐ【ぬぐ】to take off, undress
古い【ふるい】old
けれど but
急いで【いそいで】hurriedly
手【て】hand
覆う【おおう】to cover
〜ながら while
帰る【かえる】to return

　困る is used in a lot of different contexts and there is not a good English equivalent. 困った is often used to express that you are in a dilemma or embarrassed by something. Here it has been translated as "this won't do..." to express this meaning.

　In the second sentence, the post-positional phrase 自分の頭の上に modifies 被っていた.

　The third sentence uses けれど, which is a more formal version of けど, but carries the same meaning. It also shows a common alternative to the て-form: the stem-form of a verb functions the same way as a て-form, linking two phrases together with the meaning of "and;" however, this is only used in writing, not speech.

　And in the final sentence, just like with 並んで, 急いで is used adverbially to mean "hurriedly." Also, conjugating a verb with ながら indicates that the subject is intentionally doing two (or more) things simultaneously. Thus it is usually translated as "while." So the old man is simultaneously (and intentionally) covering his head with his hand and returning home.

　　　おばあさんはおじいさんが濡れて帰ってきたのを見て、びっくりしていました。
　　　「何が起こったの？おじいさんのカサはどこですか」と聞きました。
　　　おじいさんはおばあさんにおじぞうさまの話をしました。
　　　「それは良いことをしましたね。まあまあ、おモチなんて、なくてもいいですよ」

　　濡れて【ぬれて】wet
　　びっくりする is astonished, surprised
　　何【なに】what
　　起こる【おこる】to happen, occur
　　聞く【きく】to ask
　　話【はなし】をする to tell a story
　　良い【よい】good
　　こと thing, matter
　　する to do
　　まあまあ well…
　　なんて things like, such as
　　なくてもいい can do without, need not have

　　This sentence is a little complicated, but provides good practice with a few important forms of grammar. The first part to notice is the use of the の particle. It is added to the phrase おじいさんが濡れて帰ってきた so that the phrase can be used in a noun phrase slot. の can nominalize phrases in the same manner as こと (which we saw earlier). (And 濡れて is another instance of a verb acting adverbially, essentially meaning, "wetly.")

So the main sentence is simply, おばあさんは＿を見て、びっくりしていました。

In the modifying phrase, there is another pairing of a verb and the auxiliary verb くる, with a different meaning than before. In this case, くる is being used to indicate movement in space. It indicates that the motion was oriented toward the subject (or the speaker). On the other hand, when a verb is paired with いく (行く = "to go") in this way, it means that the motion was oriented away from the subject (or the speaker). (And at the end of the story, there is actually a sentence containing 帰っていった.) This difference is like the difference between saying, "came back home" (帰ってきた) and "went back home" (帰っていった).

In casual speech, questions are usually not asked with the か particle and instead use the の particle or just rising intonation. So in the sentence, 何が起こったの？, の is a (casual) question particle.

なんて is a contraction of など (which means, "etc") and とて (which means, "that kind of thing"), so it is often said to mean, "things like" or "such as" when it follows a noun, verb, or adjective. However, it often is tinged with negative feelings, so a better transliteration is probably, "or whatever" since that phrase can range from being completely neutral or laced with disdain (especially when spoken by teenagers).

おばあさんはニコニコして言いました。

おじいさんのしたことを一緒に喜びました。しかし、食べ物や飲み物がなくなってしまっていました。二人は薄い布団に包まって、早く寝てしまいました。

ニコニコする to smile
一緒に【いっしょに】together (with)
喜ぶ【よろこぶ】to rejoice, be delighted
しかし but
食べ物 food
飲み物 beverage
なくなる to run out
薄い【うすい】thin
布団【ふとん】futon
包まる【くるまる】wraps up (in a blanket)
早く【はやく】early
寝る【ねる】to go to bed, sleep

しまう is another auxiliary verb paired with the て-form of a verb to indicate that the verb was "done completely" or "finished." It is often used to express disappointment or regret that the verb was completed, but it can also just mean that the subject finished doing the verb. The nuance of regret is often open to interpretation and also often difficult to translate smoothly. There is another instance of this auxiliary verb in the second to last sentence of this story.

Cultural Note: Futons in Japan are not couches that fold out into beds. They are quilted mattresses that are laid directly on the floor for sleeping and are pliable enough that they can be folded up and stored in a closet during the day. The Western version perhaps acquired the name futon since the mattress was originally similar to the Japanese futon (although some mattresses in the Western version are cushioned with springs now).

In Japan, futons can often be seen hanging over the balcony railings of apartment buildings to air them out. They are also often beaten with what looks like a giant flyswatter to prevent the padding from clumping up.

　　その夜、激しく降る雪がますます積もりました。
　　夜中におじいさんとおばあさんはふと目を覚ましました。不思議な声が「じいさんの家はどこだ？じいさんの家はどこだ？」と歌いました。

　　夜【よる】night
　　ますます more and more, increasingly
　　夜中【よなか】midnight
　　ふと suddenly
　　目を覚ます【めをさます】to wake up
　　不思議な【ふしぎな】mysterious, strange
　　声【こえ】voices
　　歌う【うたう】to sing

　　目を覚ます and 目が覚める are expressions commonly used as the transitive and intransitive forms of "wake up." These verbs are almost never seen without 目 and 目を覚ます is actually part of the Japanese word for alarm clock: 目覚まし時計 (めざましどけい). And like the way we say just, "alarm," this word is also often abbreviated to just 目覚まし.
　　Since most Japanese words don't have plural forms, sometimes we simply have to guess whether a noun is plural or singular. Here, 声 has been translated as plural, since all the Jizou are probably singing.

その声は、にぎやかで楽しそうな歌声です。どうやら二人の家に向かってやってくるような様子です。

> にぎやかな lively
> 楽しい【たのしい】merry
> 歌声【うたごえ】singing voices
> どうやら … ような it seems like, appears that
> やってくる to come around
> 様子【ようす】aspect, characteristic

　どうやら can be used on its own to create a simile (a way of describing something by comparing it to something else), but is often paired with ような which does the same thing.

　Here we have another sentence that is just, 様子です, with the rest of the sentence being a phrase modifying 様子. 様子 is a noun meaning "aspect" or "characteristic" or, if it's something that can be seen, "appearance." The unnamed subject here is その声, the subject of the previous sentence. So the sentence is literally, "They [the voices] have the aspect of seeming to come toward the couple's house." To make the translation smoother, though, mention of the "aspect" was left out, as often happens with the word 様子, since it is somewhat implied. Here again, 向かって is acting adverbially to mean, "toward."

　Both of these sentences are in non-past tense because they provide commentary.

歌声はどんどん近づいて、とうとう二人の家の前までくると、何か重いものを置く音がしました。それから声は消えてしまいました。

 どんどん steadily
 近づく【ちかづく】approaches, draws near
 とうとう finally, at last
 まで up to, until
 くる to come
 何か【なにか】…もの something …
 重い【おもい】heavy
 置く【おく】to put down
 音【おと】がする to make a sound
 それから after that
 消える【きえる】to disappear, vanish

 The first phrase of this sentence is straightforward, but the second and third phrases contain a few different forms of grammar worth mentioning. In the second phrase, the particle まで is the counterpart to the particle から as in: 月曜日から金曜日まで働く。"[Sub] works from Monday to Friday."

 And the と following くる is the と conditional and it is used here to suggest an immediate sequence of events and is often translated, "as soon as". So this middle phrase means something like, "…as soon as they [the singing voices] came at last to the front of the couple's house…"

 In the third phrase, we encounter the combination 何か…もの. We can add verbs and adjectives between 何か and もの to make noun phrases meaning, "something…" For example, 何か食べるもの = "something to eat" and 何か新しいもの = "some-thing new."

二人はそっと戸を開けて、じっと見ていました。雪はすでに止んでいて、あたりには月の光が明るく輝きました。遠くにカサを被ったおじぞうさまが帰っていくのが見えました。
　　そして、家の前にはお正月のおモチが山のように置いてありました。

　　そっと softly, quietly
　　戸【と】door
　　開ける【あける】to open
　　じっと見る【みる】to stare
　　すでに already
　　止む【やむ】stops, ceases
　　あたり area, vicinity
　　月【つき】the moon
　　光【ひかり】light
　　明るく【あかるく】brightly
　　輝く【かがやく】to sparkle, shine
　　遠くに【とくに】in the distance
　　見える【みえる】to be visible, in sight
　　そして and
　　山【やま】mountain

　　Here we encounter 帰っていく as mentioned earlier. Remember, when a verb is paired with the auxiliary verb いく in this way, it means that the motion was oriented away from the subject.
　　In the final sentence, 山 is linked to ように. As mentioned before, ような is used to create a simile. And since it is followed by に, it has been converted into an adverb and is thus telling what the rice cakes were *piled* like: "like a mountain."
　　Also, this sentence's main verb 置く is paired with the auxiliary verb てある. When a verb is conjugated into て-form and paired with the auxiliary verb ある, instead of describing a lasting

activity (as with いる), it describes an action that resulted in a lasting state. This construction also indicates that this lasting state was done on purpose by someone (although, the actor might be unknown). For example, this auxiliary verb is often used with 予約【よやく】 "reservation," as in: コートを予約してあるから、テニスをしよう。 "I booked a court, so let's play tennis."

In each story, the rules of grammar will not be explained, over and over again. So when a rule has been explained in one story, it will not be re-explained in any of the subsequent stories. Thus the following parts of grammar will not be explained in any of the subsequent stories, since we have had practice with them in this story:

Using ような to create a simile.

Using ていく and てくる to indicate movement in space.

Using てしまう to indicate that the subject finished doing the verb (perhaps regrettably).

Using の and こと to nominalize a phrase.

Using も following each noun in a list with the meaning of "both…and…"

Using 時 to turn a phrase into an adverbial phrase meaning "when…"

Using non-past tense to provide commentary or express a character's thoughts.

Using postpositional phrases both adverbially and adjectivally.

These parts of grammar will turn up in several if not all of the following stories, so make sure these are known before proceeding onward.

子育て幽霊

　　昔々、林の近くの村にアメ屋を開いている男の人がいました。
　　ある梅雨の夜、アメ屋さんが店を閉めたところ、戸を静かに叩く音がしました。
　「へえ、こんな遅く誰なんだ？」
　と、アメ屋さんが戸を開けてみると、青白い顔をした女の人が立っていました。
　「あの、アメをください」
　と、細い声で言って、一円を差し出しました。
　「あ、はい。ちょっとお待ち下さい」
　アメ屋さんは怪しんだが、女が悲しそうな小声で頼むので、水アメのツボを取ってきました。女の人が持ってきた器に、ツボから水アメを入れてあげました。それから、消えるように帰っていってしまいました。

　　その翌日、アメ屋さんが店を閉めたところ、また戸を静かに叩く音がしました。
　「あの、アメをください」
　やはり、あの女の人でした。アメ屋さんは「どこに住んでいるのか」と尋ねようとするが、女の人は昨日と同じようにアメを買うと、スーッと、どこかへ帰っていきます。次

の夜も、その次の夜も、決まってやってきました。それから毎晩、女の人は夜遅くになる時に現れては同じようにアメを買っていくのです。

　ある雨の夜のこと。
　この日は隣村の大工が訪ねてきて、夜遅くになるまでいろんなことを話し合いました。すると、いつものように戸を静かに叩く音がしました。
　「はて、こんなとんでもない時間に...？」
　と大工は言いました。
　「お客さんですよ」
　と、アメ屋さんは言い、水アメのツボを取ってきて戸を開けました。
　「あの、アメをください」
　と、いつものように女の人は言いました。青白い顔をした女の人を見ると、大工は恐怖で震え出しました。
　「あ、あの、あの女は、僕の村の出身だけど、一ヶ月前に死んだ！」
　「えっ！本気？」
　「間違いない」
　二人は、顔を見合わせて、女の後を付けてみることにしました。アメを買った女の人は隣村へ向かったけど、中途で森に入った。二人は、ためらったが、結局森の方へ歩き出しました。その森は影を落とすと夜よりも暗くなります。二人は森を抜ける小道に入る後で、雨はだんだん激しくなりました。
　小道は細いです。だんだん暗くなります。やっと月の光に包まれる墓場に到着しました。
　「ほら！墓だ！」
　と、アメ屋さんはささやきました。
　女の人は墓に歩いていくと、スーッと煙のように消えてしまいました。
　「お化けだ！」

二人は恐怖で震え出したと、赤ん坊の泣き声が聞こえてきました。雨の中で泣き声ははっきり聞こえました。二人は、怖がっていたが、それでも声のする方へ行ってみました。

　「おお、人間の赤ん坊じゃないか！」
　と、アメ屋さんは言いました。
　赤ん坊を抱き上げるとそばに手紙が見えました。それによると、赤ん坊は捨て子でした。
　「こんな人気のないところでいったい何をしているの？」
　ふと墓の横の器を見ると
　「あっ、毎晩アメを買っていったあの女の人の器だよ！なるほど、捨て子を育てるために幽霊となったのだろう」

　感心したアメ屋さんは、赤ん坊を引き取り、育てることにしました。
　「この子は私が育てる。ご安心ください」
　それからあの女の人がアメを買っていくことは、もう二度となかったそうです。

THE CHILD-REARING GHOST

Once upon a time, there was a man who ran a candy store in a small village near the woods.

One night in the rainy season, just after the candy store owner had closed his shop, there came the sound of someone quietly knocking on the door.

"Huh? Who could it be at this hour?" the candy store owner said and when he opened the door, a pale-faced woman stood there.

"Um, may I have some candy?" she said in a thin voice, holding out one yen.

"Oh, of course. Wait one moment."

The candy store owner was dubious, but, seeing as she requested it in such a sorrowful whisper, he went to get his jar of candy syrup. The candy store owner scooped candy syrup from the jar into the bowl the woman carried. After that, she seemed to disappear as she returned home.

The next day, just after the candy store owner had closed his shop, there again came the sound of someone quietly knocking on the door.

"Um, may I have some candy?"

As expected, it was that woman. The candy store owner tried to ask where she lived, but just like the day before, she bought candy, then returned to wherever she came from in a flash. The next night and the night after that she turned up without fail. And every night from then on, the woman bought candy, always appearing late at night.

Now, one rainy night, a carpenter from a neighboring village came to visit. They talked of various things together late into the evening at which point there came the sound of someone quietly knocking on the door, like always.
"Huh? At such an unearthly hour?" the carpenter said.
"It's just a customer," the candy store owner said then fetched his jar of candy syrup and opened the door.
"Um, may I have some candy?" the woman said like always.
When the carpenter saw the pale-faced woman, he began to tremble with fear.
"Th-that-that woman comes from my village, but she died a month ago!"
"Eh! Really?"
"I'm certain."
The two men looked at each other and decided to follow after the woman. The woman who bought candy headed toward the neighboring village, but, half-way there, she entered a forest. The two men hesitated, but eventually started to walk toward the forest. That forest cast a shadow blacker than the night. After the two men entered a path that passed through the forest, the rain gradually became more intense.
The path was narrow. It became darker and darker until, at last, they arrived at a cemetery bathed in moonlight.
"Look! A grave!" the candy store owner whispered.
The woman walked to the grave, then vanished like a puff of smoke.
"A ghost!"
As the two men began to tremble in fear, they heard a baby's cry. The cry could be heard clearly over the rain. The two men were frightened, but even so went toward the voice.

"Oh, it's a human baby, isn't it?" the candy store owner said.

As soon as he picked up the baby, he saw a letter nearby. According to it, the baby was a foundling.

"What in the world are you doing in such a lonely place?"

Suddenly, they saw a bowl next to the grave.

"Oh, it's the bowl of that woman who came and bought candy each evening! I see, she became a ghost in order to raise the abandoned child."

The candy store owner admired the woman and decided to take charge of the baby and raise it.

"I will raise this baby. Please be at peace."

And it is said that, from that day on, the woman never again came to buy candy.

VOCABULARY AND GLOSS

　　昔々、林の近くの村にアメ屋を開いている男の人がいました。
　　ある梅雨の夜、アメ屋さんが店を閉めたところ、戸を静かに叩く音がしました。

　　昔々【むかしむかし】once upon a time
　　林【はやし】forest
　　近く【ちかく】near
　　村【むら】village
　　アメ candy
　　屋【や】shop (suffix)
　　開く【ひらく】to open (for business)
　　男の人【おとこのひと】man
　　ある a certain…
　　梅雨【つゆ】rainy season
　　夜【よる】night
　　アメ屋さん【あめやさん】*see below
　　店【みせ】shop
　　閉める【しめる】to close
　　ところ *see below
　　戸【と】door
　　静かな【しずかな】quiet
　　叩く【たたく】to knock, tap
　　音がする【おとがする】to make a noise

　　Here ところ does not mean "place" except in a very abstract sense. When it follows a past tense verb, it gives the meaning of "just [verb]-ed" and when it follows a present tense verb, it gives the meaning of "about to [verb]." For example, 彼は出たところだ means, "He just left," while 彼女は出るところだ means, "She is about to leave."

Cultural note:

The suffix 〜さん is can be added to the store designation to refer to someone who runs or works at that type of store. However, it can also just be used to more politely refer to that store (similar to adding お〜 or ご〜 to a noun). For example, すし屋さんに行くなんてどうですか？means, "Do you want to go to a sushi bar or something?"

「へえ、こんな遅く誰なんだ？」
と、アメ屋さんが戸を開けてみると、青白い顔をした女の人が立っていました。
「あの、アメをください」
と、細い声で言って、一円を差し出しました。

へえ (interjection of surprise)
こんな such…, like this…
遅く【おそく】late
誰【だれ】who
開ける【あける】to open
青白い【あおじろい】pale
顔【かお】face
する to wear (a facial expression)
女の人【おんなのひと】woman
立つ【たつ】to stand
あの um
ください please give me
細い【ほそい】thin
声【こえ】voice
言う【いう】to say
一円【いちえん】one yen
差し出す【さしだす】to hold out

Here we have another auxiliary verb used with て-form: みる (見る) which means "to try something out," (lit. "do [verb] and see"). In English, the word "try" can also mean "make an effort to do," like if the door was heavy and the candy store owner was going to see if he could manage to open it. However, てみる doesn't carry this meaning, it indicates that the subject *tried out* the verb without really knowing what the consequences will be. Because of the two meanings of "try" in English, the meaning of てみる is often left untranslated.

Notice here that in Japanese the way of saying "pale-faced" is more like saying, "to wear a pale face." The verb する has many other meanings besides "to do."

Besides adding auxiliary verbs after the て-form of a verb, certain auxiliary verbs can be attached directly to the stem-form of a verb. After the second quote, the auxiliary verb 出す is used in this way. In this case, we have 差す ("to hold up") combined with 出す ("to take out," "to present") to mean, "to hold out." Later in the story we will see that 出す can also add a different meaning as an auxiliary.

Note: if this story took place "once upon a time," one yen would have been expensive for candy. But since the smaller forms of currency are obsolete, I felt there was no reason to include them in a story aimed at beginner and lower intermediate readers.

「あ、はい。ちょっとお待ち下さい」

アメ屋さんは怪しんだが、女が悲しそうな小声で頼むので、水アメのツボを取ってきました。女の人が持ってきた器に、ツボから水アメを入れてあげました。それから、消えるように帰っていってしまいました。

あ oh!
ちょっと
待つ【まつ】to wait
下さい【ください】please
怪しむ【あやしむ】to be dubious, suspect
悲しい【かなしい】sad
小声【こごえ】low voice
頼む【たのむ】to request, order
水アメ【みずあめ】starch syrup
ツボ jar
取ってくる【とってくる】to fetch, go and get
持ってくる【もってくる】to bring
器【うつわ】bowl
入れる【いれる】to put in, insert
それから and then, after that
消える【きえる】to vanish
帰る【かえる】(of a customer, guest) to leave

The phrase ちょっと待って ("wait a second") is extremely common. If you've ever watched anything in Japanese or been to Japan, you've probably heard it. The phrase used by the candy store owner here is a politer version of it. Most verbs that don't have an honorific form can be conjugated into a politer form by adding the honorific prefix お to the stem form of the verb and adding になる or です after the verb. Furthermore, polite requests can be made by adding the honorific prefix お to the stem form of the verb and adding ください after the verb. So ちょっと待って changes to ちょっとお待ち下さい.

The second sentence includes several parts of grammar explained in the last story and a few new ones. The use of くる in 取ってくる indicates that the subject will go somewhere, do the verb, then return. In English, we usually say sentences like, *I will go and buy bread*, where the "coming back" is understood. In Japanese, people would say, 私はパンを買ってくる, where the "going out" is understood. So the phrases *go and get* and 取ってくる are good translations of each other even though the coming and going differ.

At the end of the second to last sentence, we have てあげる, which is a more polite version of てやる (which was seen in the last story) but has the same meaning: that the verb was done as a favor for someone else (the subject gives the doing of the verb).

　　その翌日、アメ屋さんが店を閉めたところ、また戸を静かに叩く音がしました。
　「あの、アメをください」
　やはり、あの女の人でした。アメ屋さんは「どこに住んでいるのか」と尋ねようとするが、女の人は昨日と同じようにアメを買うと、スーッと、どこかへ帰っていきます。次の夜も、その次の夜も、決まってやってきました。それから毎晩、女の人は夜遅くになる時に現れては同じようにアメを買っていくのです。

　　翌日【よくじつ】next day
　　また again
　　やはり of course, as expected
　　住む【すむ】to live, reside

尋ねる【たずねる】to ask, inquire
昨日【きのう】yesterday
と同じ【おなじ】the same as
スーッと suddenly, quickly
次【つぎ】next, subsequent
決まって【きまって】always, without fail
やってくる to come around
毎晩【まいばん】every evening
夜遅く【よるおそく】late at night
なる becomes
〜時【とき】when…
現れる【あらわれる】to show up, appear

翌 is a prefix meaning "next" or "following."

The third sentence contains the other form of "try." The volitional form of a verb followed by とする gives the meaning of "make an effort to do." Volitional + とする often implies that the subject tried and failed as it does here. The candy store owner tried to ask the woman where she lives, but received no answer.

同じ can be attached directly to a noun, like 同じクラス ("same class"); it can also be used with the particle と, like 私と同じ ("the same as me"); and it can be used in both ways, like 私と同じクラス ("the same class as me"). So 昨日と同じ means, "the same as yesterday."

スーッと is an onomatopoeic word that probably is supposed to sound like a sucking sound. And 決まって is another occurrence of a verb being used adverbially, indicating that something has become regularly occurring.

ある雨の夜のこと。
　この日は隣村の大工が訪ねてきて、夜遅くになるまでいろんなことを話し合いました。すると、いつものように戸を静かに叩く音がしました。
「はて、こんなとんでもない時間に...？」
と大工は言いました。
「お客さんですよ」
と、アメ屋さんは言い、水アメのツボを取ってきて戸を開けました。
「あの、アメをください」
と、いつものように女の人は言いました。

雨【あめ】rain
日【ひ】day
隣村【となりむら】neighboring village
大工【だいく】carpenter
訪ねる【たずねる】to visit
いろんな various
話し合う【はなしあう】to talk together
すると at which point, whereupon
いつも always
はて Oh dear! Goodness!
とんでもない outrageous, unthinkable
時間【じかん】time

　As we saw in the last story, sentences that modify こと are often used in Japanese as a way to introduce what is about to be told. And here, the copula です has been dropped from the sentence since it is "obvious" (to a native speaker). That's right, not only subjects and objects, but verbs can also be dropped from sentences in Japanese! Written out completely, this sentence would be: ある雨の夜のことです。

In the second sentence, we have another example of an auxiliary verb being attached to the stem form of a verb. When the verb 合う is attached to another verb, it adds the meaning "to do [verb] to each other" or "to do [verb] together." So 話し合う becomes "to talk together."

　　青白い顔をした女の人を見ると、大工は恐怖で震え出しました。
　　「あ、あの、あの女は、僕の村の出身だけど、一ヶ月前に死んだ！」
　　「えっ！本気？」
　　「間違いない」
　　二人は、顔を見合わせて、女の後を付けてみることにしました。

　　見る【みる】to see, observe
　　恐怖【きょうふ】fear, terror
　　震え出す【ふるえ　だす】to begin to tremble
　　僕【ぼく】I (male casual form)
　　出身【しゅっしん】a person's origin (where they're from)
　　死ぬ【しぬ】to die
　　えっ huh?
　　本気【ほんき】serious
　　間違いない【まちがいない】I have no doubt
　　二人【ふたり】two people
　　見合わせる【みあわせる】to look at each other, exchange glances
　　女の後【おんなのあと】after the woman
　　付ける【つける】to follow, shadow
　　ことにする decide to do…

Here we have yet another verb combination, 震え出す, with the other meaning of 出す. In this case, 出す means "to start" (which isn't too different in meaning from "to take out" or "present"). 出身 is a noun that is used to tell where a person is from. For example, someone might ask you, ご出身はどちらですか？ Or you could simply supply the information that, カリフォルニアの出身です.

And in the last sentence, we have another surprise ending with ことにする. This is simply an expression used to say that the subject "decides to do" the phrase that modifies こと.

アメを買った女の人は隣村へ向かったけど、中途で森に入った。二人は、ためらったが、結局森の方へ歩き出しました。その森は影を落とすと夜よりも暗くなります。二人は森を抜ける小道に入る後で、雨はだんだん激しくなりました。

向かう【むかう】to head toward
中途【ちゅうと】halfway
森【もり】woods
入る【はいる】to enter
ためらう to hesitate
結局【けっきょく】eventually, in the end
方【ほう】direction
歩き出す【あるきだす】to start to walk
影【かげ】shadow
影を落とす【かげをおとす】to cast a shadow
暗い【くらい】dark, gloomy
抜ける【ぬける】to pass through
小道【こみち】path
だんだん gradually

激しい【はげしい】intense, furious

Here again we have 出す added to another verb to make 歩き出す, where 出す adds the meaning of "start to."

In the phrase 夜よりも暗くなります, the particle より makes the phrase 夜より暗い a comparison: "darker than the night." The particle も adds emphasis like saying, "even darker than the night." And, as was pointed out in the last story, when an い-adjective is used with the verb なる, the い is replaced with く. So a transliteration of the entire sentence is something like, "When those woods cast a shadow, [it] becomes even darker than the night."

後で is used in the same way as 時に, but gives the meaning of "after [the modifying phrase]." So here it means, "After the two men entered a path that passed through the forest…"

小道は細いです。だんだん暗くなります。やっと月の光に包まれる墓場に到着しました。
「ほら！墓だ！」
と、アメ屋さんはささやきました。

やっと at last
月【つき】the moon
光【ひかり】light (natural)
包む【つつむ】to cover with, wrap up
墓場【はかば】graveyard, cemetery
到着【とうちゃく】to arrive
ほら look!
墓【はか】grave
ささやく to whisper, murmur

Here is our first instance of passive form; however, this is not the "inconvenience" passive form taught in most textbooks.

Due to exposure to English, Japanese also contains a passive form which is the same as the one in English and simply conveys that the action was done to the subject (as opposed to active sentences in which the subject does the action). So に包まれる simply means, "was covered with…" We will see more of the passive form in the next story.

ほら is used to call someone's attention to something like saying, "Look!" If you go to an aquarium or zoo in Japan you will quickly become fluent at hearing this word.

女の人は墓に歩いていくと、スーッと煙のように消えてしまいました。
「お化けだ！」
二人は恐怖で震え出したと、赤ん坊の泣き声が聞こえてきました。雨の中で泣き声ははっきり聞こえました。二人は、怖がっていたが、それでも声のする方へ行ってみました。

歩く【あるく】to walk
煙【けむり】smoke, fumes
お化け【おばけ】ghost
赤ん坊【あかんぼう】baby
泣き声【なきごえ】crying voice
聞こえる【きこえる】is audible
はっきり clearly, distinctly
怖がる【こわがる】feels scared
それでも nevertheless
行く【いく】to go

The suffix がる can be added to the stem-form of adjectives to describe how a third-party feels or what they show signs of feeling.

In Japanese, there are no strict conventions for comma use, but one common use of commas is that when a comma follows the subject marker は, it signals that the indicated subject is the subject for both phrases. So in the last sentence here, 二人は、 signals that "the two men" is the subject of each of the following phrases. In other words, the two phrases could be rewritten as 二人は怖がっていた and それでも二人は声のする方へ行ってみた.

「おお、人間の赤ん坊じゃないか！」
と、アメ屋さんは言いました。
　赤ん坊を抱き上げるとそばに手紙が見えました。それによると、赤ん坊は捨て子でした。
「こんな人気のないところでいったい何をしているの？」

人間【にんげん】human
〜じゃないか isn't it?
抱き上げる【だきあげる】to pick up and hold
そば near, beside
手紙【てがみ】letter
見える【みえる】is in sight
〜によると according to…
捨て子【すてこ】foundling, abandoned child
人気のない【ひとけのない】deserted
ところ place
いったい …on earth?, …in the world?
何【なに】what

The sentence ending じゃないか is used to question something, similar to adding "isn't it?" to the end of English sentences.

〜によると is used to cite where information came from. この本によると means "According to this book," and 予報【よほう】によると means "According to the weather forecast," etc.

いったい is an adverb that makes questions more emphatic when it comes before an interrogative word like 何, どうして, どこ, etc. So, for example, いったいどこ usually gets translated to something like, "where in the world," and いったい何 gets translated to something like, "what on earth," etc.

　　ふと墓の横の器を見ると
　「あっ、毎晩アメを買っていったあの女の人の器だよ！なるほど、捨て子を育てるために幽霊となったのだろう」
　　感心したアメ屋さんは、赤ん坊を引き取り、育てることにしました。
　「この子は私が育てる。ご安心ください」
　　それからあの女の人がアメを買っていくことは、もう二度となかったそうです。

ふと suddenly, unexpectedly
横【よこ】next to, beside
なるほど I see
育てる【そだてる】to raise, bring up
ために for
幽霊【ゆうれい】ghost
感心する【かんしんする】to admire
引き取る【ひきとる】to take care of, look after
〜ことにする to decide to do…
子【こ】child
私【わたし】I
ご安心【ごあんしん】peace of mind
もう more, further

二度と【にどと】 *see below

そう it is said that…

In the last story, we saw that ため can be linked to a noun phrase with の in order to describe the purpose of that noun phrase. It can also modify a verb phrase when it is followed by に, so here ために is being used to say she became a ghost (幽霊となった) for the purpose of raising the abandoned child (捨て子を育てる).

The use of 〜となる is similar to 〜になる, but the use of と implies that it is more of a complete change at once from one thing to another, while に is used for more natural or gradual changes.

The word 二度 means "twice," but when 二度と is paired with a negative ending (like it is here), it takes on the meaning of "never again." This is often paired with もう, which simply strengthens the assertion.

When そう is attached to a sentence, it is used to report hearsay. For example, the sentence 彼は先月死んだそうだ means, "I hear that he died last month."

雪女

　　昔々、寒い寒い北国に親子の狩猟者が住んでいました。息子の名前は明でした。
　　毎年、この親子は山がすっかり雪に被られる頃になると、狩猟に出かけていくのです。
　　ある冬の日、二人はいつものように山へ入っていって、狩猟をしました。山の奥の方に入っていくと、急に空は黒雲に覆われて、大風が吹き出しました。あいにく雪も降り始めて吹雪となりました。激しい雪にもかかわらず、なんとか小屋を見つけました。
　「今夜、ここで泊まるより、仕方がない」
　　火を起こしたが、体が暖かくなってきませんでした。まもなく、すっかり眠くなって、明の父親は眠ってしまっていました。そして、明もついウトウトとしました。
　　後で風の勢いで戸がガタンと開き、雪と一緒に人影が入ってきました。明の声は恐怖で震えていました。
　「だ、だ、誰だ？」
　　美人でした。美人は真っ直ぐ明の方へ歩いていって優しく言いました。
　「お前はまだ若々しいから、お前の体を暖めるけれど、今夜のことをもしも誰にも話したら、お前の命は終わってしまいましょう」

明は誰にも言わないと約束して、明の口から美人は白い息を吸い込みました。口から白い息は出ると、明の体はだんだん暖かくなりました。それから、美人は吹雪の中に吸い込まれるように消えてしまい、明はそのまま気を失ってしまいました。
　　翌朝、目が覚めた明は急いで父親のところに行ってみたが、父親が眠ったまま、静かに亡くなったのを見つけたのです。

　　それから一年が経ちました。
　　ある大雪の夜、誰かが戸を叩く音がしました。明は戸を開けてみると、一人の美しい娘が立っていました。
　　娘は「雪の中で道に迷ってしまいました。どうしていいか分かりません」と言いました。
　　かわいそうだと思った明は娘を家に入れてやりました。娘はユキという名前でした。その冬、ユキは明の妻になり、幸せに暮らしました。
　　また一年が過ぎました。

　　ある冬の夜のことでした。
　　明が狩猟に出かけていく間に、ユキは家で針仕事をしていました。でも、雪はだんだん激しくなったので、明のことを心配していて、嵐を見に外へ出ました。
　　大雪のために明は早く帰ってきました。家に着いた時に、ユキは戸口に立っているのを見ました。明はうっかり約束を忘れて、
　　「ユキはあの美人とそっくりだなあ」
　　とささやきました。
　　これを聞いたユキが「お前は約束を破ってしまった。その夜のことを言わなりればよかったなあ」と悲しそうに言い、吹雪の中に吸い込まれるように消えてしまいました。
　　それから、空気が大変寒くなって、寒い空気を吸い込むと、明はもうすっかり冷たくなってしまっていました。

THE SNOW WOMAN

Once upon a time, in the cold, cold northlands, there lived a hunter and his son. The son was named Akira.

Every year, around the time when the mountains were completely covered with snow, this father and his son would set out hunting.

One winter's day, the two entered the mountains like always and went hunting. As soon as they passed into the depths of the mountain, the sky suddenly was covered with black clouds and a gale began to blow. Unfortunately, snow also started falling and whipped up into a blizzard. In spite of the fierce snow, though, they somehow found a small hut.

"We have no choice but to spend the night here."

They built a fire, but it didn't make them any warmer. Soon they became overwhelmed by drowsiness and Akira's father nodded off. And, against his will, Akira also dozed off.

Later, the force of the wind banged the door open and a figure entered the room along with the snow. Akira's voice shook with fear.

"Wh-wh-who's there?"

It was a beautiful woman. She walked straight toward Akira and gently said, "Since you are still young, I will warm you, but if you ever speak of this night, your life will, regrettably, end."

Akira promised not to tell anyone and the beautiful woman inhaled the frosty breath from Akira's mouth; as he breathed out, his body gradually warmed. Then the beautiful woman disappeared as though she had been sucked out into the blizzard and Akira passed out.

When he woke the next morning, Akira rushed to his father only to discover that his father had quietly passed away in his sleep.

One year later, on a day of heavy snow, there came the sound of someone knocking on the door. When Akira went to see who it was, a lone, beautiful girl was standing there.

The girl said, "I lost my way in the snow. I don't know what to do."

Akira felt sorry for the girl and brought her in his house. The girl was named Yuki and that winter, she became Akira's wife and they lived happily.

Another year passed.

One winter's night, while Akira was out hunting, Yuki did some needlework at home. But, because the snowfall became heavier and heavier, she became worried and went outside to look at the storm.

Akira came home early because of the heavy snow. When he arrived, he saw Yuki standing in the doorway. Inadvertently, he forgot his promise and murmured, "Yuki looks just like that beautiful woman…"

When she heard this, Yuki said sorrowfully, "You broke your promise…I wish you had not spoken of that night," and disappeared as though she had been sucked out into the blizzard.

Then the air became frigid and as soon as he sucked in the cold air, Akira turned to ice.

VOCABULARY AND GLOSS

　昔々、寒い寒い北国に親子の狩猟者が住んでいました。息子の名前は明でした。
　毎年、この親子は山がすっかり雪に被られる頃になると、狩猟に出かけていくのです。

　　昔々【むかしむかし】once upon a time
　　寒い【さむい】cold
　　北国【きたぐに】north country
　　親子【おやこ】parent and child
　　狩猟者【しゅりょうしゃ】hunter
　　住む【すむ】to live, reside
　　息子【むすこ】son
　　名前【なまえ】name
　　明【あきら】Akira
　　毎年【まいねん】every year
　　山【やま】mountain
　　すっかり completely, thoroughly
　　雪【ゆき】snow
　　被る【かぶる】to be covered with
　　頃【ころ】approximate time, time of year
　　なる becomes
　　狩猟【しゅりょう】hunting
　　出かける【でかける】to set out, go out

　北国 and 親子 are compound nouns. Words like these are very common and we will see more in the next paragraph and a few more throughout the rest of the story. A lot of the time, the meaning of the two words will simply be combined: 北国 = "north" + "country" and 親子 = "parent" + "child." But note that the initial consonant of the second word is sometimes changed as in 北国:「きた＋くに」→「きたぐに」.

Another compound word that can be seen in every train station is the word for "exit": 出口(でぐち). And in bigger stations, the exits might be divided into 北口(きたぐち), 東口(ひがしぐち), etc.

Note here that the verb 被る which we saw in カサじぞう is now used with the meaning of "to be covered with" instead of "to put a hat on." It is also in passive form, so the verb is done to the subject (山).

ある冬の日、二人はいつものように山へ入っていって、狩猟をしました。山の奥の方に入っていくと、急に空は黒雲に覆われて、大風が吹き出しました。

ある冬の日【あるふゆのひ】one winter's day
二人【ふたり】two people
いつも always
入る【はいる】to enter
奥【おく】interior
方【ほう】direction
急に【きゅうに】suddenly
空【そら】sky
黒雲【くろぐも】black clouds
覆う【おおう】to cover, conceal
大風【おおかぜ】strong winds
吹き出す【ふきだす】to spurt out

These sentences contain excellent practice of the grammar concepts covered in the previous stories. And here the passive form of 覆う perhaps expresses inconvenience, but the nuance of annoyance is often open to interpretation and also often difficult to translate smoothly.

53

あいにく雪も降り始めて吹雪となりました。激しい雪にもかかわらず、なんとか小屋を見つけました。
　　「今夜、ここで泊まるより仕方がない」

あいにく unfortunately
降り始める【ふりはじめる】starts to precipitate
吹雪【ふぶき】blizzard
激しい【はげしい】fierce, violent
〜にもかかわらず in spite of, nevertheless
なんとか somehow
小屋【こや】hut, cabin
見つける【みつける】to spot, come across
今夜【こんや】tonight
泊まる【とまる】to take shelter in, spend the night in
〜より other than, except
〜仕方がない【しかたがない】…it's no use

　　When 始める is used as an auxiliary verb, it has the expected meaning of, "starts to."
　　Here we have another instance of 〜となる (instead of 〜になる), which indicates that the change happened all at once to reach a final stage—a blizzard.
　　かかわる is a verb meaning "influences," "affects," etc, and the ending ず is the classical form of なくて with the same meaning; the も particle is added for emphasis, like the word "even." So the phrase にもかかわらず literally means, "is not even influenced/affected by…and…" However, it is usually translated into the much smoother sounding, "in spite of…" For example, 私は雨にもかかわらず出かけた。= "I went out in spite of the rain." ("I was not even influenced by the rain and went out.") It is a common expression.
　　Akira's father uses another expression, より仕方がない, in the last sentence here. This phrase is easy to understand once

we divide it into parts. 仕方 is a noun meaning "means," "method," "way," etc. For example, 料理の仕方 is "the way/method of cooking" ("how to cook") and 車の運転の仕方 is "the way/method of driving a car" ("how to drive a car"). So the expression 仕方がない (literally, "there is no way/means") is used to indicate that "it's no use" doing [the rest of the sentence]. And, in this grammar, the particle より is present, which we know is used to mark one side of a comparison, so 〜より仕方がない indicates that "it is no use doing anything other than…" the option marked with より. Or more smoothly, "We have no choice other than…"

火を起こしたが、体が暖かくなってきませんでした。まもなく、すっかり眠くなって、明の父親は眠ってしまっていました。そして、明もついウトウトとしました。

　　火【ひ】fire
　　起こす【おこす】to cause
　　火を起こす build a fire
　　体【からだ】body
　　暖かい【あたたかい】warm
　　まもなく soon, before long
　　眠い【ねむい】sleepy, drowsy
　　眠る【ねむる】to sleep
　　つい unintentionally, against one's better judgment
　　ウトウトとする to doze off

　　Both 眠る and 寝る(ねる) mean "to sleep," but with 眠る the subject does not necessarily have to be lying down (they could be sleeping in a chair, etc), while 寝る indicates the subject is lying down but does not necessarily have to be sleeping.

風の勢いで戸がガタンと開き、雪と一緒に人影が入ってきました。明の声は恐怖で震えていました。
　　「だ、だ、誰だ？」

　　風【かぜ】wind
　　勢い【いきおい】force
　　戸【と】door
　　ガタン (slamming sound)
　　開く【あく】opens
　　一緒に【いっしょに】together with
　　人影【ひとかげ】figure of a person
　　声【こえ】voice
　　恐怖【きょうふ】fear
　　震える【ふるえる】trembles
　　誰【だれ】who

　　一緒に is an adverb indicating that the subject performed the verb "together with" another noun. The other noun is marked with the と particle (unless it is obvious from context and omitted). So in the phrase 雪と一緒に美人が入ってきました, the subject 美人 (marked with the が particle) came inside (入ってくる) together (一緒に) with the snow (雪と).

美人でした。美人は真っ直ぐ明の方へ歩いていって優しく言いました。
「お前はまだ若々しいから、お前の体を暖めるけれど、今夜のことをもしも誰にも話したら、お前の命は終わってしまいましょう」

美人【びじん】beautiful woman
真っ直ぐ【まっすぐ】directly, straight for
歩く【あるく】to walk
優しい【やさしい】kind, gentle
言う【いう】to say
お前【おまえ】you (casual)
まだ still
若々しい【わかわかしい】youthful, young
暖める【あたためる】to warm, heat
今夜【こんや】tonight, this night
〜のこと of…
もしも if
誰にも【だれにも】anyone
話す【はなす】to speak, tell
〜たら if
命【いのち】life, lifespan
終わる【おわる】ends, finishes

Adding 〜のこと to a noun is the same as adding "of" or "about" in English, like in, "thinking of you" (君のことを考えている).

Because verbs come at the end of the phrase in Japanese, there is sometimes an adverb near the beginning of the phrase to give a hint about the verb's conjugation. もしも is one such adverb that indicates the verb is going to be conjugated into a conditional form. However, it cannot stand alone—although it sort of means "if," the verb that follows it must be conjugated into a conditional form.

たら is sometimes referred to as the past conditional, because it is used to say that after the phrase preceding たら happens, then the clause following it will happen. So the beautiful woman is essentially saying that if Akira speaks of that night to anyone, then, after he speaks of it, his life will end.

Note that 終わる is intransitive, so the beautiful woman is not saying that *she* will end Akira's life but that his life will come to an end. And this paragraph ends with ましょう, which is the volitional form of the ます ending. However, this phrase does not mean, *"Let's end your life." Volitional form can be used not only to make suggestions, but also to express an intention or determination. For example, in the sentence 明日君に電話しよう, the speaker is saying, "I will call you tomorrow." So, in a sense, the phrase お前の命は終わってしまいましょう means, "your life (regrettably) intends to come to an end."

明は誰にも言わないと約束して、明の口から美人は白い息を吸い込みました。口から白い息は出ると、明の体はだんだん暖かくなりました。
　それから、美人は吹雪の中に吸い込まれるように消えてしまい、明はそのまま気を失ってしまいました。
　翌朝、目が覚めた明は急いで父親のところに行ってみたが、父親が眠ったまま、静かに亡くなったのを見つけたのです。

約束【やくそく】promise
口【くち】mouth
白い【しろい】white
息【いき】breath
吸い込む【すいこむ】to inhale, breathe in
出る【でる】leaves, exits
だんだん gradually
それから after that, and then
中【なか】in, inside
消える【きえる】vanishes, disappears
そのまま as it is, without change
気【き】mind, consciousness
失う【うしなう】to lose, part with
気を失う to lose consciousness, faint
翌朝【よくあさ】the next morning
目が覚める【めがさめる】to awaken
急いで【いそいで】hurriedly
ところ place, spot
行く【いく】to go
〜まま as it is, without change
静かに【しずかに】peacefully
亡くなる【なくなる】to pass away, die

The verb 約束 can use the quoting particle と in the same way as the verbs 言う, 思う, etc.

The verb 込む is another verb commonly used as an auxiliary verb. It usually adds the meaning of "into" as in "to go into" or "to put into," so it is sort of the opposite of 出す.

まま is used to express a lack of change. It is technically a particle, but it is used just like a noun. We first see it as そのまま in the phrase 明はそのまま気を失ってしまいました. Here it indicates that Akira lost consciousness "without changing" anything else. In other words, he didn't lie or sit down or brace himself, etc. Then まま follows a verb in the phrase, 父親が眠ったまま, which indicates that Akira's father "did not change" from sleeping. In other words, he remained asleep and did not wake up (he died in his sleep).

Cultural Note:

まま is actually used by store clerks to ask if you would like a bag. They may ask, このままでよろしいでしょうか？ which literally means, "Is it okay as it is?" (よろしい is a politer version of いい). In other words, the clerk is asking if you want to take the merchandise without a bag.

On the other hand, if the clerk reaches for a bag and you don't want one, you can say, このままでだいじょうぶです。

それから一年が経ちました。
　ある大雪の夜、誰かが戸を叩く音がしました。「へえ、こんな遅くに誰だろうか」と思いながら戸を開けてみると、一人の美しい娘が立っていました。

　　一年【いちねん】one year
　　経つ【たつ】passes, lapses
　　大雪【おおゆき】heavy snow
　　夜【よる】night
　　誰か【だれか】someone
　　叩く【たたく】to knock, tap
　　音【おと】がする to make a sound
　　へえ (surprised interjection)
　　こんな such a, like this
　　遅く【おそく】late
　　誰【だれ】who
　　思う【おもう】to wonder, think
　　開ける【あける】to open
　　一人【ひとり】lone (one person)
　　美しい【うつくしい】beautiful, lovely
　　娘【むすめ】girl, daughter
　　立つ【たつ】stands

　The verb 経つ is used to refer to the passage of time and not objects (like a car, airplane, etc).
　だろうか is the casual version of でしょうか and basically has the same meaning as だ except with uncertainty added. So 誰だろうか, basically means, "who is it I wonder?"
　娘 can mean one's own daughter, but it is also used to mean "girl."

娘は「雪の中で道に迷ってしまいました。どうしていいか分かりません」
　　　かわいそうだと思った娘を家に入れてやりました。娘はユキという名前でした。
　　　その冬、ユキは明の妻になり、幸せに暮らしました。
　　　また一年が過ぎました。

　　道に迷う【みちにまよう】to lose one's way
　　どうして in what way
　　いい good
　　分かる【わかる】to become known
　　かわいそう poor, pitiable
　　家【いえ】house
　　入れる【いれる】to let in, take in
　　妻【つま】wife
　　幸せな【しあわせな】happy
　　暮らす【くらす】to live
　　また again
　　過ぎる【すぎる】passes by

　　The question particle か can be used to embed a question phrase in a sentence. The か particle follows the embedded question phrase which should be in plain form and contain a question word like 何, いつ, どうして, etc. どうして is usually translated as "why" or "how," but can also mean "what way/reason." So どうしていいか means something like, "what way is good," or more smoothly, "what to do" (in plain form, there is no need for the copula だ after an adjective). The phrase どうしていいか分からない is actually a very commonly used phrase meaning, "I don't know what to do."
　　Note here that かわいそう does not mean, "looks/seems cute." And the な-adjective 幸せな is made into an adverb by replacing な with に.

ある冬の夜のことでした。
　明が狩猟に出かけていく間に、ユキは家で針仕事をしていました。でも、雪はだんだん激しくなったので、明のことを心配していて、嵐を見に外へ出ました。
　大雪のために明は早く帰ってきました。家に着いた時に、ユキは戸口に立っているのを見ました。明はうっかり約束を忘れて、
　「ユキはあの美人とそっくりだなあ」
とささやきました。

～間に【あいだに】while…
針【はり】needle, pin
仕事【しごと】work, job
針仕事【はりしごと】needlework
でも but
心配【しんぱい】worry
嵐【あらし】storm
見る【みる】to look, watch
外【そと】outside
のために because of, due to
早く【はやく】early
帰る【かえる】to return home
着く【つく】to arrive at
戸口【とぐち】doorway
うっかり carelessly, inadvertently
忘れる【わすれる】to forget about
そっくり looks just like, the spitting image of
ささやく whispers

　Like 時, the noun 間 can create a time-related adverbial. It is used to indicate that the phrase following 間 happens while the phrase modifying 間 is happening. This is a little different from ながら, which indicates that the subject is intentionally doing two (or more) things simultaneously, because with 間 the subject of each phrase can be different.

　　Here we have another example of 〜のこと and it should be clear that Yuki is "worrying about Akira." And the following sentence contains another instance of ために; however, in this case ために indicates a cause instead of a purpose. So ために is being used here to say Akira returned home early (早く帰ってきた) because of the heavy snow (大雪のために).

　　The noun そっくり is used to say that the subject of the sentence looks just like the noun that is indicated by the と particle (the に particle can also be used instead of と or even no particle at all in casual speech).

　　なあ is a drawn out version of the sentence ending particle な.

これを聞いたユキが「お前は約束を破ってしまった。その夜のことを言わなければよかったなあ」と悲しそうに言い、吹雪の中に吸い込まれるように消えてしまいました。
　それから、空気が大変寒くなって、寒い空気を吸い込むと、明はもうすっかり冷たくなってしまっていました。

聞く【きく】to hear
破る【やぶる】to break (promise, rule)
〜ばよかったなあ I wish…
悲しい【かなしい】sad, sorrowful
吹雪【ふぶき】blizzard
空気【くうき】air
大変【たいへん】very
寒い【さむい】cold
もう soon, shortly
冷たい【つめたい】cold, icy

　〜ばよかったなあ is a sentence ending used to express regret. The final verb is conjugated into ば-form and よかったなあ (or just よかった) is added. This ending literally means, "If [phrase] happened, it would have been good, wouldn't it…" So the sentence その夜のことを言わなければよかったなあ means, "I wish you hadn't spoken of that night…" ("If you didn't speak of that night, it would be good, wouldn't it…")

　After the quotation there is an い-adjective conjugated with a そう ending, which turns 悲しそう into a な-adjective. And な-adjectives can be made into adverbs by replacing な with に. So 悲しそうに modifies 言う, meaning "Yuki said, sounding sad."

　大変 can be an adverb or a な-adjective. As an adverb, it means, "very" and as an adjective, it can mean, "great/immense," "grave/terrible," or "difficult/hard." So we have to be on our toes with this word. When it comes directly before an adjective, though, we can be pretty certain it has the meaning, "very."

猫の茶わん

　　昔、古物を売っている男の人がいました。でも、田舎に行って、老人を甘い言葉にだまし、老人の古物を安く買うという、ずるい男です。
　　ある日、山にある茶店で休んでいました。男の人はお茶を飲みながら、美しい景色を眺めていました。山は緑で、空気はすばらしいです。
　　茶店を経営しているおばあさんが一匹の猫を飼っていました。男の人は猫が庭で歩き回っているのをぼんやりと見ました。猫は茶わんの前で止まって食べ始めました。男の人はそれを見て驚きました。その茶わんは何ともすばらしいのです。
　　「このばあさん、茶わんの値打ちが知っていないんだ。だから、甘い言葉にだまして、手に入れる」と思いました。
　　そこで、男の人は猫のそばへ近寄ると、その頭を撫でながらニコニコして言いました。
　　「なんて、かわいい猫だなあ。何よりも猫が大好きだ。実にすばらしい猫だ」
　　「そうですか？一日中ブラブラしている、何もしない猫ですよ」
　　とおばあさんは言いました。
　　「いやいや。猫は利口そうだ。それに、毛はとてもきれいだ。猫を飼っていることはない…なんなら、この猫を引き取らせてくれないか？」
　　「まあ、家族みたいなので、ちょっと無理でございます。でも、かわいがってくれるなら、あげてもいいですよ」

おばあさんの言葉に、男の人はやったと思いました。後は猫と一緒に、あの茶わんもつけてもらえばいいのです。
　「それで、いくらで猫を売ってくれるかな？」
　「そうですね。猫のことですから高くもいえませんが、十万円で売りましょう」
　「はっ？十万円も！」
　ところが、あの茶わんはあれよりもずっと高価です。
　「わかった」
　男の人は財布から十万円を取り出して、おばあさんに渡しました。
　（今が一番大切な時間だ）
　と、思いました。
　「ところで、ついでにこの茶わんも持っていくよ。新しい皿より食べ慣れた皿の方が、猫も喜ぶと思うので」
　おばあさんはきっぱり断りました。
　「いいえ、茶わんをさしあげられません」
　「どうして。ただの古い器」
　男の人は何度も頼みましたが、おばあさんは絶対に茶わんを与えませんでした。
　やっと、おばあさんは言いました。
　「これは、私の一番大事な宝物ですから！」
　男の人は怒り出して、声を張り上げて叫びました。
　「大事な宝物なら、なんで猫の皿なんかにするんだ！」
　「言いたくなければ、言う必要はない！猫を持って、すぐに出発してください」
　男の人は猫を抱いて茶店を出ました。でも、猫が好きではないので、外に捨てました。
　猫は急いで茶店へ戻っていきました。
　「よし。また戻ってきたね」
　おばあさんは茶わんで猫に餌を与えて、何度も頭を撫でてやりました。
　「この茶わんのおかげで、何回もお前を売れるね」

THE CAT'S TEACUP

Long ago, there was a man who sold antiques. But he was a sly kind of man who goes to the countryside to deceive elderly people with honeyed words and buy their antiques for next to nothing.

One day, he took a break at a tea shop in the mountains. While the man was sipping his tea, he gazed at the beautiful scenery: the mountains were green and the air was fresh and clean.

The old woman who ran the tea shop had a cat and the man absentmindedly watched the cat walk around in the garden. The cat stopped in front of a tea cup and began to eat. The man was astonished when he saw this, because that tea cup was exquisite.

"It must be that this old woman doesn't know the value of that tea cup. So I'm going to deceive her with sweet words and get my hands on it."

Accordingly, the man went up to the cat and, while petting its head, he smiled and said,

"What a cute cat! I love cats more than anything in the world! It's a truly splendid cat."

"You think so? He's a cat that lazes around all day doing nothing," the old woman said.

"No no. He seems well-behaved. Besides, his coat is lovely. I have never had a cat…if you are so inclined, won't you let me adopt this cat?"

"Well, he is like family, so it's a little unreasonable. But if will give him lots of love, I can give him to you."

At the old woman's words, the man thought, I've done it! Because all he has to do now is to get the woman to include that tea cup with the cat.

"And at what price will you sell him to me for?"

"Well, since he's a cat, I can't say something expensive, but I will sell him for one hundred thousand yen."

"Huh? *One hundred thousand* yen!"

However, that tea cup was worth more than even that by far.

"Alright."

The man took out one hundred thousand yen from his wallet and handed it over to the old woman.

Now is the most critical moment, he thought.

"While you are at it, I'll take this tea cup, too. Because I think cats also are happier with the bowl they are used to eating from than with a new bowl."

The old woman flatly refused.

"No, I cannot give you that tea cup."

"Why? It's just an old bowl."

The man asked her over and over, but the old woman absolutely would not give it to him.

Finally, the old woman said, "Because this is my greatest treasure!"

The man lost his temper and shouted at the top of his voice, "If it's a great treasure, then why in the world do you use it as a cat's bowl!"

"If I don't want to say, I don't have to say! Please take your cat and leave immediately."

The man picked up the cat and left the tea shop. But, since he didn't like cats, he abandoned it outside.

The cat hurried back to the tea shop.

"Good, you returned again, huh?"

The old woman gave the cat some food in the tea cup and pet his head over and over.

"Thanks to this tea cup I can sell you over and over, can't I?"

VOCABULARY AND GLOSS

　　昔、古物を売っている男の人がいました。でも、田舎に行って、老人を甘い言葉にだまし、老人の古物を安く買うという、ずるい男です。

　　昔【むかし】once upon a time
　　古物【ふるもの】antiques
　　売る【うる】to sell
　　男【おとこ】man
　　人【ひと】person
　　でも but
　　田舎【いなか】countryside, "the sticks"
　　行く【いく】to go
　　老人【ろうじん】elderly people
　　甘い言葉【あまいことば】honeyed words, flattery
　　だます to deceive, cheat
　　安い【やすい】cheap
　　買う【かう】to buy
　　ずるい sly, sneaky

　　The second sentence uses という to modify 男 in a way that is probably unfamiliar. It can be thought of as being similar in meaning to "to call," just like with 明という人. So 田舎に行って、老人を甘い言葉にだまし、老人の古物を安く買うという男 is like saying, "a man you would call, 'someone who goes to the countryside to deceive elderly people with honeyed words and buy their antiques for next to nothing.'" So there is a subtle difference between this usage and the same sentence with という removed similar to the difference between saying, "the kind of man who goes to the countryside…" and just, "a man who goes to the countryside…"

ある日、山にある茶店で休んでいました。男の人はお茶を飲みながら、美しい景色を眺めっていました。山は緑で、空気はすばらしいです。

ある日【あるひ】one day
山【やま】mountains
茶店【ちゃみせ】tea house
休む【やすむ】takes a break, rests
お茶【おちゃ】green tea
飲む【のむ】to drink
美しい【うつくしい】beautiful
景色【けしき】scenery, landscape
眺める【ながめる】to view, gaze at
緑【みどり】green
空気【くうき】air
すばらしい fresh and clean, splendid

Note that the use of で here after 緑 is the て-form of です.

茶店を経営しているおばあさんが一匹の猫を飼っていました。男の人は猫が庭を歩き回っているのをぼんやりと見ました。猫は茶わんの前で止まって食べ始めました。

　　経営する【けいえいする】to manage
　　おばあさん old woman
　　一匹【いっぴき】one (animal)
　　猫【ねこ】cat
　　飼う【かう】to keep (a pet)
　　庭【にわ】garden
　　歩き回る【あるきまわる】to walk to and fro
　　ぼんやりと idly, casually
　　見る【みる】to watch
　　茶わん【ちゃわん】tea cup
　　前【まえ】front, before
　　止まる【とまる】to stop
　　食べ始める【たべはじめる】start to eat

　　The word to use for "I have a..." when speaking of a pet is 飼う. This is much more common than using いる. ぼんやり is an adverb with several different meanings, but here it is used with the meaning, "idly" or "casually." The cat is probably also walking around idly, but here it is modifying 見る (so it is the man that is doing something idly). It can stand alone or be followed by と and/or する.

　　The second sentence uses an auxiliary verb that we have not seen yet: 回る, which adds the meaning, "to go around." Other examples include 飲み回る "to go on a pub crawl" and 見回る "to patrol, make one's rounds."

男の人はそれを見て驚きました。その茶わんは何ともすばらしいのです。
　　　「このばあさん、茶わんの値打ちが知っていないんだ。だから、甘い言葉にだまして、茶わんを手に入れる」と思いました。
　　　そこで、男の人は猫のそばへ近寄ると、その頭をなでながらニコニコして言いました。

驚く【おどろく】is surprised, astonished
何とも【なんとも】extremely
すばらしい exquisite, splendid
ばあさん less respectful version of おばあさん
値打ち【ねうち】value
知る【しる】*see below
だから therefore
手に入れる【てにいれる】to obtain
思う【おもう】to think
そこで so, therefore
そば near
近寄る【ちかよる】approaches
頭【あたま】head
なでる to pet, stroke
ニコニコする to smile
言う【いう】to say

　　　Japanese contains several verbs with a "built in" meaning of "to become" or "to get" etc. The verb 知る is one example and means "to come to know" and not just "to know." We could use 知る to say something along the lines of "I come to know world events from the news." But when we want to say we know something or someone, we have to use 知っている. It's like saying, "I have come to know and continue knowing."

「なんて、かわいい猫だなあ。何よりも猫が大好きだ。実にすばらしい猫だ」
　　「そうですか？一日中ブラブラしている、何もしない猫ですよ」
　　とおばあさんは言いました。

なんて What…!
かわいい cute, adorable
何よりも【なによりも】more than anything
大好き【だいすき】really like, love
実に【じつに】truly, absolutely
そうですか？is that so?
一日中【いちにちじゅう】all day long
ブラブラする to be lazy, idle
何も【なにも】nothing
する to do

　　The word なんて acts as an intensifier when it is used at the beginning of a sentence. It gives a meaning similar to "What…" or "How…" as in なんてきれいな山だ！("What a beautiful mountain!").

　　There aren't strict rules for comma usage in Japanese grammar, but when a comma is put in between two modifying phrases, it means that they both modify the following noun. So in this case, the two phrases 一日中ブラブラしている and 何もしない both modify 猫. And when 何 is followed by も and a negative verb, it takes on the meaning of "nothing," so 何もしない means, "does nothing."

「いやいや。猫は利口そうだ。それに、毛はとてもきれいだ。猫を飼っていることはない…なんなら、この猫を引き取らせてくれないか？」

「まあ、家族みたいなので、ちょっと無理でございます。でも、かわいがってくれるなら、あげてもいいですよ」

いや no
利口【りこ】well-behaved
それに and, besides
毛【け】fur
とても very
きれい beautiful, lovely
なんなら if you are so inclined
引き取る【ひきとる】to adopt
くれる to give (to me)
まあ well…
家族【かぞく】family
ちょっと a little
無理【むり】unreasonable, impossible
かわいがる to love, be affectionate to
てもいい *see below

For those not familiar with honorifics, でございます is the humble version of です. The old woman is talking politely since the man is a customer, while he speaks in casual form. In fact, the old woman uses polite form until the very end when she talks to her cat and even uses it when she becomes angry.

Adding もいい to the て-form of a verb is used for granting and requesting permission to do the verb. For example, the sentence 一緒に行ってもいいですか means, "May I go with you?" This is because adding ても to a verb gives it the meaning of "even if," so the previous sentence literally means, "Even if I go with you, is it okay?" And in the story, あげてもいいです

means, "even if I give it to you, it is okay," or, more smoothly translated, "I can give it to you."

　　おばあさんの言葉に、男の人はやったと思いました。後は猫と一緒に、あの茶わんもつけてもらえばいいのです。
　「それで、いくらで猫を売ってくれるかな？」
　「そうですね。猫のことですから高くもいえませんが、十万円で売りましょう」
　「はっ？十万円も！」

やった Hooray!
後は【あとは】after this
一緒に【いっしょに】together with
つける to include, add
ばいい *see below
それで and, thereupon
いくら how much
かな "I wonder"
そうですね Well...
高い【たかい】expensive
十万円【いちまんえん】100,000 yen (~$900)

　　When もらう follows the て-form of a verb, it functions in a similar way to て and て, but means, "to receive the favor of someone doing" or "to get someone to do." So in the second sentence, 猫と一緒に、あの茶わんもつけてもらう means, "to get the old woman to include that tea cup together with the cat." Now, when the ば-conditional is followed by いい, it means something along the lines of "all you have to do is..." so the complete sentence becomes, "All he has to do after this is to get the woman to include that tea cup."
　　In the last sentence, the man says, 十万円も．The も particle here is used with a meaning like "as much as." It is the

77

opposite of using しか（＋ない）．For example, 一円しか持っていない。 means, "I only have one yen." On the other hand, 彼は猫を五匹も飼っている。 means something like, "He has *five cats*!" Numbers do not require a particle (beyond the counter), so these particles are used to emphasize/comment on the numbers. In a sense, both particles indicate that the number they follow is unusual.

ところが、あの茶わんはあれよりもずっと高価です。
「わかった」
男の人は財布から十万円を取り出して、おばあさんに渡しました。
（今が一番大切な時間だ）
と、思いました。

ところが however
ずっと by far, much
高価【こうか】high price
わかった alright, sure
財布【さいふ】wallet
取り出す【とりだす】to take out
渡す【わたす】to hand over, give
今【いま】now
一番【いちばん】*see below
大切【たいせつ】important
時間【じかん】time

The word 一番 can be added to adjectives as a qualifier, giving them the meaning of "the most" or "the best." For example, 一番いい means, "the best (most good)" and 一番おいしい means, "the most delicious." It is used in this way again later in the story.

「ところで、ついでにこの茶わんも持っていくよ。新しい皿より食べ慣れた皿の方が、猫も喜ぶと思うので」
　おばあさんはきっぱり断りました。
「いいえ、茶わんをさしあげられません」
「どうして。ただの古い器」

ところで by the way
ついでに while you are at it
持っていく【もっていく】to take
新しい【あたらしい】new
皿【さら】dish, plate
食べ慣れる【たべなれる】to be used to eating
喜ぶ【よろこぶ】to be delighted, pleased
きっぱり flatly, decisively
断る【ことわる】to reject, turn down
さしあげる to offer, give (polite)
どうして why
ただ just, only
古い【ふるい】old
器【うつわ】bowl

　In the second sentence we have another new auxiliary verb: 慣れる, which adds the meaning, "to grow accustomed to." Other examples include, し慣れる, "to get used to doing" and 見慣れる "to become used to seeing."
　Note that the second sentence is incomplete, because it ends in ので. This sentence should actually be the beginning of the first sentence (and be followed by a comma), but it is common in spoken Japanese for elements that normally come at the beginning of the sentence to be said after the sentence. This seems to happen most often with the subject.

男の人は何度も頼みましたが、おばあさんは絶対に茶わんを与えませんでした。
　　やっと、おばあさんは言いました。
　　「これは、私の一番大事な宝物ですから！」
　　男の人は怒り出して、声を張り上げて叫びました。

何度も【なんども】many times over
頼む【たのむ】request, beg
絶対に【ぜったいに】absolutely
与える【あたえる】to give
やっと at last
私の【わたしの】my
大事【だいじ】valuable, important
宝物【たからもの】treasured item
から because
怒り出す【おこりだす】to lose one's temper
声【こえ】voice
張り上げる【はりあげる】to raise (one's voice)
叫ぶ【さけぶ】shouts

　　In the last sentence, the phrase 声を張り上げて is acting adverbially in the usual way, but since there is no "raised-voicedly" adverb in English, it has been translated as, "at the top of his voice," which carries the same meaning.

「大事な宝物なら、なんで猫の皿なんかにするんだ！」
「言いたくなければ、言う必要はない！猫を持って、すぐに出発してください」
　男の人は猫を抱いて茶店を出ました。でも、猫が好きではないので、外に猫を捨てました。
　猫は急いで茶店へ戻っていきました。
「よし。また戻ってきたね」
　おばあさんは茶わんで猫にえさを与えて、何度も頭をなでてやりました。
「この茶わんのおかげで、何回もお前を売れるね」

なら if
なんで why
なんか things like
必要【ひつよう】a necessity, need
持つ【もつ】to carry, take
すぐに immediately
出発する【しゅっぱつする】to depart
抱く【だく】to hold in the arms
出る【でる】leaves
好き【すき】to like
外【そと】outside
捨てる【すてる】abandon
急いで【いそいで】hurriedly
戻る【もどる】to return
よし good
また again
えさ feed (animal)
おかげで thanks to…
何回も【なんかいも】time and time again
お前【おまえ】you (informal)

The beginning of the phrase 言いたくなければ、言う必要はない！ might look a little confusing at first because several conjugations are combined. The first is 言いたい, meaning "want to say." Now, verbs conjugated into たい-form are used and conjugated like い-adjectives, so to negate 言いたい, we change the い to く and add ない. So 言いたくない means, "don't want to say." But this is conjugated again into ば-form, in which instead of changing the final い to く, the い is replaced with けれ and ば is added. And this is just the usual ば-conditional, so 言いたくなければ means, "If I don't want to say."

大工と三毛猫

　　昔、江戸に一人の大工が住んでいました。彼は結婚して幸せに暮らしていました。
　　ある年のこと、妻はミケ猫がほしいと知らせました。そこで、大工は猫を買いに出かけましたが、どこにも見つけられませんでした。彼は来る日も来る日も探しました。あいにく、ミケ猫を見つける前に、妻は病気になっていました。医者に診てもらったけど、医者の努力はむなしくて、妻はまもなく死んでしまいました。
　　葬式の後で、大工は一人で歩いて帰りました。やがて、一匹のミケ猫を連れてやってくることに気付きました。妻が亡くなって、とても寂しかった大工は、猫を飼っていることにしました。
　　そのミケ猫をまるで自分の子のようにかわいがていました。大工は毎朝、お手洗いに行くより先に猫のご飯を用意します。猫も大工のことが大好きで、来る日も来る日も大工が帰る時に暖かく迎えてあげるのでした。
　　ところが大工の視力は弱くなっていて、大工仕事が下手になりました。とても貧乏になるのを心配しました。そこで、医者を相談すると、「残念ですが、目を治すのは私の力に余る仕事です。それはとてもできません」と、言うのです。

　　その夜、大工は帰って、ミケ猫に向かって言いました。

　　「なあ、俺の視力は弱くなってしまって、治りそうもない。どうしたらいいだろう？」

大工は猫に話しかけているうちに、ウトウトしてしまいました。ミケ猫は、まるで何でも理解するように、「ニャー」と鳴くと、大工に近寄って、彼の目を何度も舐め始めたのです。それに気づいた大工は、「奇妙だが、気持ちがいい」と思って、再び眠りに落ちました。

　　翌朝、大工の目はすっかり治って、前よりはるかによく見えます。おかげで、大工仕事が上手になって、素晴らしいものをたくさん作りました。手伝ってくれたお礼に、毎日大工はミケ猫に新鮮な魚を買ってあげるようにしました。
　　それからはずっと幸せに暮らした。

THE CARPENTER AND THE CALICO CAT

Once upon a time in Edo, there lived a carpenter who was happily married.

One year, his wife told him she wanted a calico cat. So the carpenter went out to buy one, but couldn't find one anywhere. Day after day he searched. Unfortunately, before he could find a calico cat, his wife became sick. They went to see a doctor, but the doctor's efforts were futile and his wife soon died.

After the funeral, the carpenter was walking home alone. Before long he noticed a calico cat accompanying him. The carpenter, who was very lonely from his wife's passing, decided to keep the cat.

He loved that calico cat as though it were his own child. Every morning, before he even went to the bathroom, the carpenter would prepare the cat's food. The cat also loved the carpenter and, day in and day out, gave him a warm welcome when he came home.

However, the carpenter's eyesight was becoming weak and his carpentry became clumsy. He worried that he would become very poor, so he consulted a doctor, who said, "It's regrettable, but healing your eyes is a task beyond my ability. I can't possibly do it."

That night, the carpenter returned home and said to the calico cat,

"Say, my eyesight has weakened and it's unlikely that it will get better. What should I do?"

While speaking to the cat, the carpenter nodded off. As though she understood everything, the calico cat meowed as she went to the carpenter and began licking his eyes over and over again. When the carpenter noticed it, he thought, "It's strange, but feels good," and fell back asleep.

The next morning, his eyes were completely healed and he could see much better than before. Because of that, his carpentry improved and he made many wonderful things. To thank her for her help, the carpenter made a habit of buying fresh fish for the calico cat every day.
    And they lived happily ever after.

VOCABULARY AND GLOSS

　昔、江戸に一人の大工が住んでいました。彼は結婚して幸せに暮らしていました。
　ある年のこと、妻はミケ猫がほしいと知らせました。そこで、大工は猫を買いに出かけましたが、どこにも見つけられませんでした。

昔【むかし】once upon a time
江戸【えど】Edo
一人【ひとり】one person
大工【だいく】carpenter
住む【すむ】to live
彼【かれ】he
結婚する【けっこんする】to be married
幸せ【しあわせ】happy
暮らす【くらす】to live
ある年【あるねん】one year
妻【つま】wife
ミケ猫【みけねこ】calico cat
ほしい to want
知らせる【しらせる】to inform
そこで so
買う【かう】to buy
出かける【でかける】to go out
どこにも nowhere
見つける【みつける】to find, locate

　In the second sentence, 結婚して is acting adverbially, which should be very familiar by now and 幸せに暮らした is a common collocation meaning, the subject "lived a happy life." For example, "they lived happily ever after," can be written, それから はずっと幸せに暮らした as it is at the end of the story.

Historical Note:

Edo is the former name of Tokyo; it was renamed in 1868. However, it was not always the capital of Japan. The home of the Emperor is traditionally held to be the capital and from 794 to 1868, the Emperor lived in what is now Kyoto (it was called Heian-kyo then).

The character 京【きょう】 means capital and is in the names for both 東京【とうきょう】 and 平安京【へいあんきょう】 東 is the character for "east" and 平安 means, "tranquility," so Tokyo literally means, "eastern capital" and Heian-kyo means "tranquil capital."

彼は来る日も来る日も探しました。
　あいにく、ミケ猫を見つける前に、妻は病気になっていました。医者に診てもらったけど、医者の努力はむなしくて、妻はまもなく死んでしまいました。

来る【くる】to come
日【ひ】day
探す【さがす】to search for
あいにく　unfortunately
前に【まえに】before
病気【びょうき】illness
なる to become
医者【いしゃ】doctor
診る【みる】to examine (medically)
努力【どりょく】effort
むなしい futile, ineffective
まもなく soon
死ぬ【しぬ】to die

　The phrase 来る日も来る日も might seem a little hard to decipher at first, but if we remember what も…も… means, it should be easier. Basically, the meaning of 来る日も来る日も is, "a day comes and another day comes," which in smoother language could be translated as "day after day."

　The word 診る is essentially the same word as 見る (見る can also mean "to examine" and they both have the same pronunciation), but the 診 kanji is used when the examining is of a medical nature. Clearly there is no way to tell these words apart in speech except through context.

葬式の後で、大工は一人で歩いて帰りました。やがて、一匹のミケ猫を連れてやってくることに気付きました。妻が亡くなって、とても寂しかった大工は、猫を飼っていることにしました。
　　そのミケ猫をまるで自分の子のようにかわいがていました。

葬式【そうしき】funeral
後で【あとで】after
一人で【ひとりで】alone
歩く【あるく】to walk
帰る【かえる】to return home
やがて before long
一匹【いっぴき】one animal
連れる【つれる】to accompany
気付く【きづく】to notice
亡くなる【なくなる】to pass away
とても very
寂しい【さびしい】lonely
飼う【かう】to keep (a pet)
ことにする decide to do
まるで as though, as if
自分の【じぶんの】one's own
子【こ】child
かわいがる to love, be affectionate to

　　The entire phrase 妻が亡くなって、とても寂しかった modifies 大工. And if we think of 妻が亡くなって as meaning, "being that his wife passed away," this phrase is easier to understand.
　　まるで is another adverb used to give a hint about the following conjugation like we saw with もしも in 雪女. When it is used this way, it indicates that a よう conjugation or a みたい conjugation is coming after it.

90

自分 is sometimes used as the word for "I" in old stories like those of Natsume Soseki. More generally, though, it means "oneself," so 自分の carries the meaning, "one's own." As you would expect, this is sometimes hard to translate since saying "oneself" and "one's own" sound very stiff in English.

大工は毎朝、お手洗いに行くより先に猫のご飯を用意します。猫も大工のことが大好きで、来る日も来る日も大工が帰る時に暖かく迎えてあげるのでした。
　　　ところが大工の視力は弱くなっていて、大工仕事が下手になりました。とても貧乏になるのを心配しました。そこで、医者を相談すると、「残念ですが、目を治すのは私の力に余る仕事です。それはとてもできません」と、言うのです。

毎朝【まいあさ】every morning
お手洗い【おてあらい】bathroom
行く【いく】to go
先に【さきに】earlier (than), before
ご飯【ごはん】meal
用意する【よういする】to prepare
大好き【だいすき】to love
帰る【かえる】returns (home)
時に【ときに】when…
暖かい【あたたかい】warm
迎える【むかえる】to welcome
ところが however
視力【しりょく】eyesight
弱い【よわい】weak
心配する【しんぱいする】to worry (about)
相談する【そうだんする】to consult
残念【ざんねん】regrettable
目【め】eye
治す【なおす】to cure, heal
私の【わたしの】my
力【ちから】ability, power
余る【あまる】to be in excess
仕事【しごと】task
とても *see below
できる can do

言う【いう】 to say

When the word とても is followed by a verb in negative form, it means "can't possibly (verb)" instead of "very." For example, とても歩かない means, "can't possibly walk."

Note: you may be familiar with the word あまり, which is derived from 余る.

Cultural Note:

In Japanese workplaces, how late you stay is very significant. Staying late signifies your dedication and enjoyment of the job. And there is a saying to use when you need to leave before your co-workers: お先に失礼します。失礼【しつれい】 means "discourtesy" and 失礼します is used for saying, "excuse me." But 先に, curiously, can be used on its own to mean "to leave before you" because the "leaving" is implied. 先 has many different usages and meanings, but to understand the above usage of 先に and its usage in the story, we just need to know that it indicates that something is done before something else. When there is a より, the order is straightforward, but sometimes, as in お先に失礼します, the order has to be uncovered from implication.

その夜、大工は帰って、ミケ猫に向かって言いました。

「なあ、俺の視力は弱くなってしまって、治りそうもない。どうしたらいいだろう？」

大工は猫に話しかけているうちに、ウトウトしてしまいました。ミケ猫は、まるで何でも理解するように、「ニャー」と鳴くと、大工に近寄って、彼の目を何度も舐め始めたのです。それに気づいた大工は、「奇妙だが、気持ちがいい」と思って、再び眠りに落ちました。

その夜【そのよる】that night
向かう【むかう】to face toward
なあ Hey, say
俺【おれ】I (masc.)
治る【なおる】recovers, gets better
そうもない very unlikely to…
どうしたらいい what should I do
話しかける to speak to
うちに while
ウトウトする to doze off
まるで as though
何でも【なんでも】everything
理解する【りかいする】to understand
ニャー meow
鳴く【なく】to make a noise (animal)
近寄る【ちかよる】approaches
何度も【なんども】many times
舐め始める【なめはじめる】start to lick
気づく【きづく】to notice
奇妙【きみょう】strange, odd
気持ちがいい【きもちがいい】a good feeling
再び【ふたたび】again, twice
眠り【ねむり】sleep

落ちる【おちる】falls

　The conjugation そうもない is just the usual そう with も added for emphasis and negated so that it conveys the meaning that something *doesn't* "look like" the property of the preceding stem-form word. However, this phrase only follows verbs, so it is a way of saying that the verb is very unlikely to happen (the use of も strengthens the unlikeliness).
　Conjugating a verb into たら-form followed by いい literally means, "it would be good if (verb)." So the phrase どうしたらいい is literally, "It would be good if I do in what way?" or in smoother language, "What should I do?"

翌朝、大工の目はすっかり治って、前よりはるかによく見えます。おかげで、大工仕事が上手になって、素晴らしいものをたくさん作りました。手伝ってくれたお礼に、毎日大工はミケ猫に新鮮な魚を買ってあげるようにしました。
　　それからはずっと幸せに暮らした。

 翌朝【よくあさ】the next morning
 すっかり completely
 はるかに by far
 いい good
 見える【みえる】to be visible
 おかげで because of…, thanks to…
 上手【じょうず】skillful
 素晴らしい【すばらしい】wonderful, amazing
 もの things
 たくさん many, a lot
 作る【つくる】to make
 手伝う【てつだう】to help
 お礼【おれい】gratitude
 毎日【まいにち】every day
 新鮮【しんせん】fresh
 魚【さかな】fish
 ようにする to be sure to…
 それから and then, after that
 ずっと the whole time

　　When いい is used adverbially, it is changed to よく (not *いく). And, if you know the difference between "good" and "well" in English, you should have no problem with these two forms.
　　The よう in ようにする means "appearance" or "manner," so ようにする literally means "do toward the appearance/manner." It's a way of saying, "to be sure to" or "to make sure to" do something. For example, 毎日運動【うんどう】するようにする means, "I make sure to exercise every day."